FROM HEAD TO SOUL

A DAILY GUIDE TO PERSONAL STYLE AND INNER SELF CONFIDENCE

FOR MEN

By Joyce Knudsen, Ph.D.

Illustrations and design by Zora Bacon
Cover illustration by Michael Clark
Editing by A. Holland

SECOND EDITION

Library of Congress Control Number: 2001091114

ISBN# 0-9701744-1-1

Knudsen, Joyce, Ph.D.
From Head to Soul
www.imagemaker1.com

Copyright 2001 Revised Edition by Joyce Knudsen, Ph.D.
The ImageMaker, Inc. Franklin, TN

PRINTED IN THE UNITED STATES OF AMERICA BY
Morris Publishing • 3212 East Highway 30 • Kearney, NE 68847
1-800-650-7888

How you feel about yourself affects how you relate to yourself, others, and ultimately what you will achieve in life. This step-by-step book is intended to help you bring your outside appearance and your inside qualities together for internal and external perfection.

Joyce Knudsen

FOREWORD

It was the early 1970s. I was fresh out of school working in the men's department at J.C. Penney when our first shipment of leisure suits arrived... I almost laughed out loud. Since then, we've seen trends come and go, from white disco suits with black shirts, to the Seattle "grunge" look, from Ross Perot's strict dress code at EDS, all the way to "business casual". Isn't it interesting that throughout these fashion swings, those who have commanded positions of leadership in business, politics and many other areas within the public spotlight seem to have remained committed to a more traditional standard of dress.

Today, my client base consists primarily of businesses who wish to utilize my services, on camera, to instruct employees in properly performing their job functions. As a corporate trainer, I am usually required to dress in a manner that emulates the presidents of their respective companies. The reason for this is obvious: it sends a message that commands respect and credibility.

I met Dr. Joyce Knudsen some ten years ago when she was running her successful business, The ImageMaker, in Rochester, Michigan. I was impressed at how she could take people from all walks of life and ages and infuse them with the confidence that they could achieve their goals and make dreams become reality. I was also honored that she allowed me to be a part of that process by utilizing my skills to provide instruction for maximizing their effectiveness on camera.

In today's world, where decisions are made at the speed of a mouse-click, and our news is given to us in 15 second sound-bytes, the need to make a favorable impression quickly is critical. In her book, From Head to Soul, Dr. Knudsen has given us a road map to follow in creating a positive image that can lead to the attainment of our goals and life's dreams. For anyone aspiring to produce an above-average lifestyle for themselves, I believe this book is a necessary ingredient.

Reavis L. Graham
Corporate Trainer
Revman Communications

TABLE OF CONTENTS

ACKNOWLEDGMENTS

My deepest thanks and appreciation go to my wonderful husband Alan, and my two very special children, Kristen and Justin, who together gave me the confidence, encouragement, and support I needed to reach my goals. Without them, this book may not have been written.

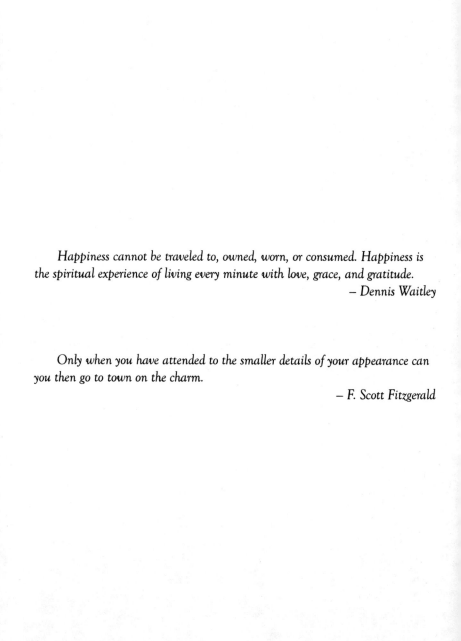

Happiness cannot be traveled to, owned, worn, or consumed. Happiness is the spiritual experience of living every minute with love, grace, and gratitude.
— Dennis Waitley

Only when you have attended to the smaller details of your appearance can you then go to town on the charm.
— F. Scott Fitzgerald

INTRODUCTION

You are very special, with unique characteristics that no one else possesses. The purpose of this "how to" book is to help you get to know who you are, to help you achieve "your individual new look," and to show you how you can become the best you can be. A positive attitude, an understanding of your unique characteristics, and an appreciation of your own uniqueness and strong points are worthy goals to strive for.

In order to be successful in life, we need to be emotionally well, physically fit, and spiritually sound. Whatever you age or profession, this book can be your daily guide to looking and feeling good about yourself.

It is a misconception to think that only people in certain positions or social situations need to look good. Many people walk around feeling unsure of themselves and probably feel that they are alone in these feelings. This simply is not true. We are all unsure of ourselves at one time or another depending on the circumstances. We are influenced by childhood experiences, peers, school, the environment, and the family. If we get positive acceptance from the things we do, we develop self confidence in these areas. If we get negative feedback from the things we do, we develop a lack of self confidence in these areas. If you acquire self acceptance within yourself, you will have the ability to accept others; if you feel self rejection within yourself, you will not be able to accept others. Self acceptance thus equals acceptance of others, whereas self rejection equals rejection of others.

Looking good on the outside is what makes people want to look inside to see what you are all about. The outside "shell" is the packaging for what lies within. The tongue can be untruthful, but the body acts with instinct. No matter how confident or sure of yourself you try to appear, you will always project how you feel about yourself on the inside. If you do not feel good about yourself physically or mentally, you will not make a good impression.

SELF-IMAGE is an attitude, believing in yourself and in what you can do. You earn self confidence when you achieve. Here are some elements to consider for a strong development of self image.

1 • POSITIVE THINKING

You can control what you say and what you feel. A positive attitude will give you the best opportunity for positive results. One positive thought a day can be the beginning of an attitude that will continue to keep you moving in a strong upward direction.

2 • STRONG SELF BELIEF

We are all unique and need to do what we feel is right, no matter how someone else feels about it. We have power over ourselves and do not need to let words or opinions of other people change the way we feel about ourselves. If you do what someone else wants you to do, you are not being yourself. Of course, in business, there are times when you may want to compromise. However, it is okay to be assertive, not aggressive, and say what you feel. Many times, if you do not say anything, the situation can get worse. And, in normal circumstances, the problem is not as difficult as you originally thought!

3 • FORTITUDE

Reach for what you want and get what you want. It is within your power to achieve the goals you set for yourself. Many famous historians, authors, and artists were not thought of as talented by the outside world. But these people believed in themselves, set a goal, and had the fortitude to persist. Thomas Edison, considered to be a dunce until he was ten, tried endlessly to invent the lightbulb and did not give up. And although Hank Aaron broke Babe Ruth's record of lifetime home runs, he also struck out 1383 times. You can do what you want to do as well.

3 • PERSONAL DEVELOPMENT

Each of us has a mental picture of ourselves—a self image—which controls much of how we act and think. To find life reasonably satisfying, you need a self image that you can live with. You must be acceptable to youself before you can be acceptable to others. Trust and believe in the self you are. You can begin to do this by following these steps:

• Develop your strengths. Make a list of all the things you are good at and read these out loud daily. You were born with unlimited potential. Believe in your abilities. Happiness and success are a choice, an attitude, and always up to you.

• Know what you are capable of. What haven't you done that you could be doing? According to William James, the average person uses only 10% of their potential. Why not expand your dreams? Dreams make plans come true.

• Write down what you want to achieve. Unless you make the choice, decide you want it, and visually look at it on paper, chances are you will not achieve your goal. If you "look" at your dream and work toward it, there is no doubt that you can do it. Of course, you must be realistic in what you set forth to do. Your goal and achievements must be within reach.

• See yourself doing it! If you have been told you could not do something, it is difficult to erase past programming. However, if you take a picture, either in your mind or an actual photograph, of what you want to achieve, you are on your way to getting there.

• Create a new person for the next new year. You can do it! If you put yourself in the frame of mind that you have already made achievements, you are almost there. It is a self-fulfilling prophecy. Self-confident people do positive things and earn self-confidence in the process. They have a clear sense of who they are and what they want. They are achievers and are always successful in life. The way you see yourself is the very projection of how others will see you.

Looking your best through hairstyles, skin care and fashion is essential to building a strong self esteem and confidence. Looking your best makes you feel good, and when you feel good, you can accomplish more. However, deeper than your outside appearance is your inner soul-the innermost part of you that must feel good. Your body will function at its best if you have your internal and external image in balance.

The goal of this book is to give you a sense of knowing the main signs of nonverbal communication. How you look to others is over 90% based on this form of communication. You will now have a guide to what others are deciding about you, based on the way you choose to look. While in the business world, external image is important, I felt it necessary to also bring in the inner self. A business professional will get so much further ahead if that professional understands image, because people will see that you care about yourself and about them. This book is a "must" for first impressions, but know that your internal image will always come through.

It's no exaggeration to say that a strong positive self-image is the best possible preparation for success in life.

— Dr. Joyce Brothers

Within you right now is the power to do things you never dreamed possible. This power becomes available to you just as soon as you can change your beliefs.

— Maxwell Maltz

As a man thinketh, he becomes.

— The Bible

You cannot always control circumstances but you can control your own thoughts.

— Charles Pepplestown

The future belongs to those who believe in the beauty of their dreams.

— Eleanor Roosevelt

If you can dream it, you can do it!

— Walt Disney

7

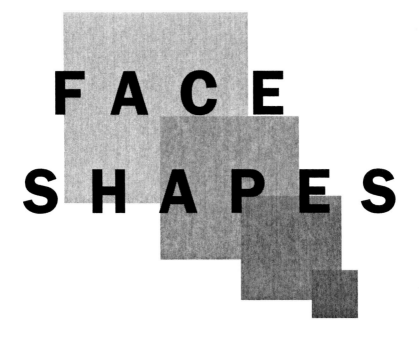

FOUR BASIC FACE SHAPES

To work with and benefit from this book, the first thing necessary to determine is your facial shape. To determine your individual facial shape, pull your hair away from your face and observe. Does your face have a squared-off appearance? Does your face seem round? Does your face appear long? Or does your face appear wider in the cheek area and taper off in the chin area?

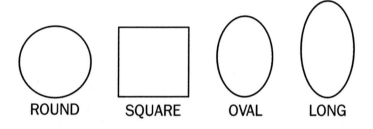

ROUND   SQUARE   OVAL   LONG

The goal in determining facial shape is to balance your look. The oval facial shape can adapt to any hairstyle. The other shapes—square, round, and long—can appear to be oval by the use of balance.

The following pages contain a detailed guide to choosing hairstyles for your particular facial shape. There will be incorrect and correct applications. Note the differences and how the "after" drawing shows balance in the facial shape.

ROUND

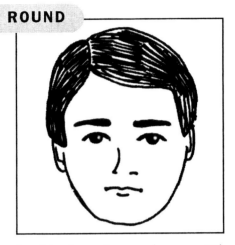

The length and width of your face are the same. When hair is pulled back away from the face, your face appears to be rounded.

SQUARE

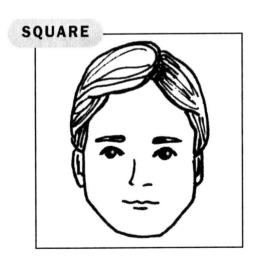

The length and width of the face are about the same, but the face is more squared-off.

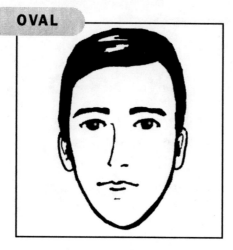

OVAL

The widest part is in the area of the cheekbone. This face shape tapers off from the cheekbone to the chin and can be considered "egg-shaped." This face can also be long from chin to forehead.

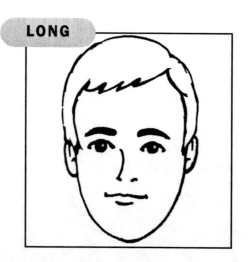

LONG

This facial shape is similar to the square except that the facial shape is slightly longer from top to bottom.

HAIRSTYLES

There are no right haircuts, only wrong ones.

— Author Unknown

Your hairstyle should balance your facial shape. A man with an oval face can wear most styles. Taller men can have fuller hairstyles and a man with a square facial shape needs to stay away from a center part. It is all a matter of balance.

The hairstyle you choose is an expression of your personality. It is important to know that an impression will be made by the hairstyle you choose.

ROUND

A round facial shape has full cheeks and chin with a rounded forehead. This facial shape requires a shorter cut put forward onto the face for added texture and volume. What this does is move the eye away from the roundness of the face. You can wear a medium length hairstyle with height and benefit from a side part.

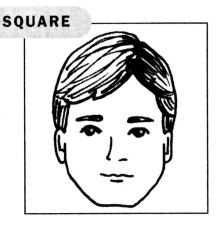

SQUARE

A square facial shape has wide cheekbones, squared forehead and jaw. This facial shape has a straight hairline. A short cut styled forward onto the face takes the eye away from the squareness. A short or medium cut looks best with some height. Choose a style that hugs the hairline.

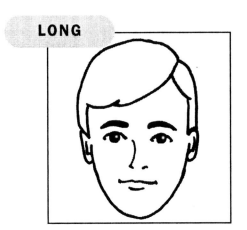

LONG

A long facial shape has a large distance between the forehead and chin. It is best to keep the height at a minimum and style hair forward onto the face to give the illusion of a smaller forehead.

OVAL

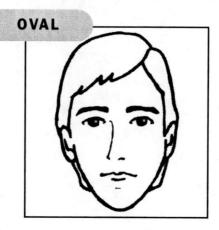

An oval facial shape can generally wear any style unless the oval tends to look more oblong, in which case you will want to balance out this facial shape. Keep your hairstyle from making your face appear too long.

A HAIRY SITUATION

There are some mistakes I have observed that I feel need mentioning. When the hairline is receding, often it starts at the temples and creates a widow's peak. But men tend to hide this by combing their hair straight across the forehead from one side to the other in a line. This is calling more attention to the problem! Instead, have the hair cut according to the natural growth pattern and try to emphasize the face asymmetrically by keeping the temple high on one side and combing the hair across to the other side, avoiding a well-defined hairline.

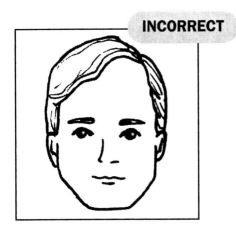

INCORRECT

CORRECT

Another common mistake is when men tease or back comb their hair and spray it to hold in place. A good stylist can help to give you a positive result. An example of a hair balding challenge is:

THE BANGS

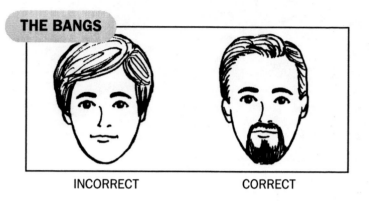

INCORRECT   CORRECT

The incorrect look obviously is trying to cover up a problem. Why call attention to it? The correct drawing illustrates how following the natural hairline, and in this case, adding a mustache and beard, give this man distinction and style. Keep your beard and hair color the same.

THE LONG STORY

It is not going to make you look like you have more hair if you grow your hair long. The shorter the hair, the better it will stand up, and the more hair you will appear to have. Weighted length only pulls the hair down and makes it weaker.

SPECIAL FEATURES AND HAIRSTYLE SELECTION

NOSE

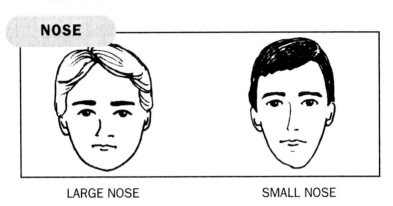

LARGE NOSE   SMALL NOSE

If your nose is either large or small, hair length becomes important. This can also influence a decision to add a beard or mustache. If the nose is large, short hair will make the nose appear larger. If the nose is thin, the face recedes even further with long hair. In both cases, it is always good to have some hair brushed across the forehead to add some diversion.

FOREHEAD

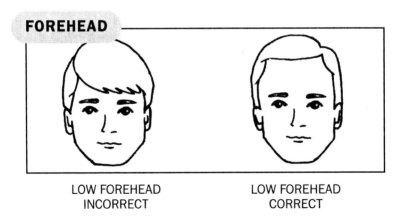

LOW FOREHEAD   LOW FOREHEAD
INCORRECT   CORRECT

If your forehead is too high or low, proper styling is imperative. If your growth is low, you should never comb your hair onto your face. If your forehead is high, styling the hair forward onto the forehead takes away some of the length.

COVER UP

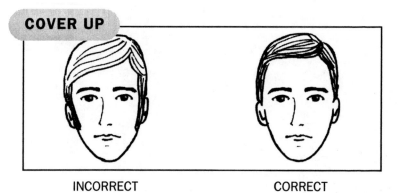

INCORRECT   CORRECT

If you train a few hairs to cover your forehead and add sideburns to show you have hair, you will be treating your balding as a disadvantage. Instead, cut the hair you have shorter and look neat and well-groomed. Lightening the hair a shade lighter is great for appearing as though you have more hair; however, you need to condition daily if you choose this route. Also, if you really want to have fuller hair, a permanent works wonders. But only have one if your stylist says your hair can handle it and you plan to take the time your hair will need to care for it.

HOW TO CHOOSE A HAIR STYLIST

It is extremely important to find a stylist that will work with you. Before you go to a stylist, be sure that you know your facial shape and that you have considered your special features, such as nose and forehead. It is perfectly acceptable to look through magazines to find a facial shape similar to yours with a hairstyle that is flattering. Ask your stylist if your hair is the correct texture to do the style.

Always determine the time it will take you to maintain your hairstyle choice. It is part of your total impression. If you do not spend the needed time on your hair, people may wonder if you will spend needed time on other things as well. Be sure to talk to your stylist on a regular basis. If your stylist does not want to consult with you about your needs as far as a hairstyle is concerned, it is time to find a stylist who will. Be sure to maintain your selection of hairstyle with regular trims and conditioning treatments.

NUTRITION AND YOUR HEALTH

A WORD ABOUT NUTRITION

Destiny shapes our ends, but calorie intake is what shapes our middles.
— Author Unknown

While it is important to choose the right hairstyle, to give your body a head to soul boost, there is no better image basic than to provide a plan for what you eat. A well balanced diet puts shine in your hair, sparkle in your eyes, and a glow to your skin. You will look better, and you will feel better about yourself.

Combine proper nutrition with exercise. Consult your physician first to see if you can put yourself on an exercise program for at least 45 minutes, 3 times a week. According to the book *Fit For Life* by Harvey and Marilyn Diamond, "for the body cycles to function effectively, it is imperative to integrate the outlined principles of good eating habits with a well balanced exercise program." Choose swimming, tennis, jumping rope, bike riding, walking, jogging or aerobic classes, but do something! It will enhance your beauty and make you feel great!

JUST RIGHT?

- Exercise 30 minutes at least three times a week.
- Check weight and measurements often to assure control.
- Eat three balanced meals a day.
- Drink 6-8 glasses of water a day.

OVERWEIGHT?

- Exercise 30 minutes each day.
- Set a goal to lose 2-3 pounds a week.
- Eat three balanced meals a day. Cut food intake in half.
- Drink 6-8 glasses of water a day.
- Keep busy.
- Stop eating before you are full.
- Chew your food thoroughly and eat slowly.
- Do not use much salt in foods. It slows down weight loss.
- Consult your physician.

UNDERWEIGHT?

- Exercise leisurely.
- Eat three balanced meals a day with mid-morning and mid-afternoon snacks.
- Eat more slowly and chew your food thoroughly.
- Rest before and after meals to allow for easier digestion.
- Keep warm on cold and windy days.
- Have a malt or protein shake daily.
- Add jam to bread and butter; butter to vegetables; rich dressing to your salads; gravy and cream sauces to meats and vegetables.
- Don't be discouraged. Weight gaining is slower than losing.
- Learn to slow down. Rushing keeps weight down.
- Consult your physician.

THE FOOD PYRAMID

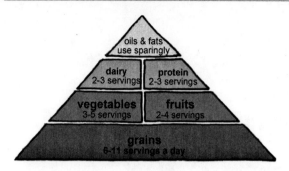

The United States Department of Agriculture has seen the benefits of using the Food Pyramid. Listed in the Journal of The American Medical Association, there was a study done over a twelve year period with 42,000 U.S. people that showed that those whose diets most resembled the pyramid had the lowest risk of dying from any cause. The statistics discovered were a 40% lower cancer risk, a 33% lower heart disease risk and a 42% lower stroke risk.

The pyramid gives you a diet low in fat and sugar and gives you complex carbohydrates, protein, fiber, vitamins, and minerals.

Here are suggested servings for each category:
- Grains: 1/4 cup cooked rice or pasta or one slice of bread.
- Produce: one cup of raw vegetables (1/4 cup if cooked) or fruit.
- Protein: 3 to 4 ounces of meat, chicken or fish, 1.5 cooked beans, or 3 eggs.
- Dairy: one cup yogurt or milk.

For additional information, go to www.usda.gov.cnpp. If you log on to this site, the government will tell you how your pyramid reads. If you enter everything you eat for one day, you will get a result of how you are doing compared with the standard.

Eating healthy and exercising three times a day for twenty minutes, or enough time to work up a sweat, will help you feel better and live longer.

SKIN CARE

Your skin is the largest organ in the body and is 90% water. The other components that make up the skin are collagen and protein. Skin is extremely important. It eliminates waste and helps to maintain body temperature. In order to properly take care of our skin, we must be on a daily skin care program which consists of cleansing, toning, and moisturizing.

DAILY CLEANSING ROUTINE

• **CLEANSING**

Cleansing removes dirt, pollution, and dead surface cells.

• **TONING**

Toning stimulates and tightens pores and cleans what the cleanser left behind.

• **MOISTURIZING**

Moisturizing returns moisture lost in the first two processes and seals in the skin's natural moisture.

Be sure your hands and your towel are clean. Pull your hair away from your face. Apply cleanser. Never rub the skin. Rinse thoroughly and pat dry with a towel. Apply toner to balance out the skin's pH. Then protect the skin with a moisturizer.

**This skin care program is just as important
for men as it is for women!**

SKIN TYPE

Your skin type is either dry, oily, or combination. It is determined by looking at your skin and seeing where the skin looks translucent and where it looks oily. If the T-zone (the forehead, nose, and chin) appears oily, you have combination skin. Be sure to go to a reputable store, such as a department store, and inquire about products that are specifically made for your skin type.

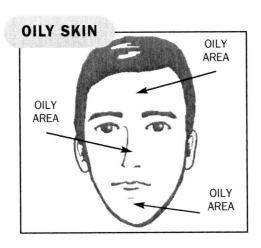

OILY SKIN

OILY AREA

OILY AREA

OILY AREA

Oily skin keeps your skin young; however, it needs special attention. It is a misconception that putting a strong astringent on this skin type will stop the problem of oily skin. If the epidermis becomes too dry, then the dermis underneath may actually cause the skin to become more oily. It is like putting the dermis into shock. You can use an astringent with a low alcohol content. This skin type will benefit from glycerin soap or herbal soap, milky cleansers and mild facial soaps. To moisturize, use an oil-absorbing mask and a mild facial scrub once a week.

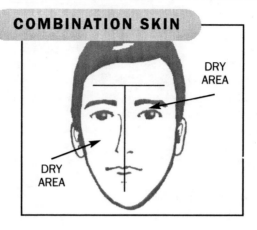

COMBINATION SKIN

DRY
AREA

DRY
AREA

Combination skin is oily down the T-zone and dry around the eye and cheek area. To cleanse your face, you need to do what is indicated for oily skin in the oily areas and what is indicated for dry skin in the dry areas. To moisturize, use cream on the dry areas and non-greasy products on the oily areas. To condition this skin type, use an astringent mask, such as lemon or pear, or slightly moisturizing yogurt masks.

DRY SKIN

Dry skin has a tendency to flake and chap. It is sensitive to the elements, such as cold and dry air, wind, and sun. This type of skin rarely has breakouts, since the pores are small. Dry skin requires some oil to make it smooth. Choose a natural glycerin soap or a cleansing cream for this skin type. Follow with a toner that does not contain any alcohol and complete with moisturizing cream to help keep natural oils in your skin. Consider a product with a built-in SPF to protect skin from daily sun damage.

SKIN COMPOSITION

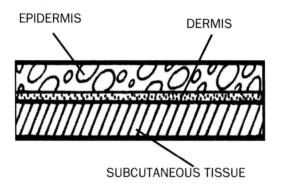

EPIDERMIS   DERMIS

SUBCUTANEOUS TISSUE

• **EPIDERMIS**

The top layer is made of keratinized protein which protects the skin from dryness and bacteria. The lower layers of the epidermis are the new cell manufacturing sites. As cells grow, they push toward the surface of the skin. They have completed their cycle by the time they reach the top of the skin. They have become dead protein. These need to be removed daily by thorough cleansing.

• **DERMIS**

The dermis lies beneath the epidermis and is where trouble begins. The dermis forms the support system of the skin. This layer contains oil, sweat glands, hair follicles, blood vessels and fat glands. The dermis is also where collagen is found, which is a type of support for the face.

29

NAIL CARE

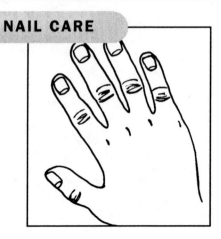

Well-groomed nails are essential for a business person. Hands are a part of your total appearance—a very important part—because the first gesture of a business person is a handshake. Your hands must be at their best. If you cannot have a weekly manicure, you can take care of your nails by scrubbing them with a nail brush and pushing back the cuticles with an orange stick. Buff and, if desired, put a low-gloss clear polish on to protect the nails. Keep your nails neatly trimmed. Nails should all be about the same length.

TEETH

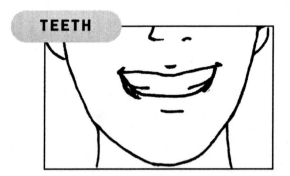

Within the first minute of meeting someone, your teeth will be noticed. If you have crooked teeth, you will look unprofessional. Bringing your mouth to attractiveness may be expensive and time consuming, but it tells others you care about yourself. If your teeth look good, you will smile more and people will know you care. See a reputable dentist and discuss how you can have the most attractive teeth possible.

EYEWEAR

Stop hiding behind those frames... have glass class! Choose a face-flattering frame in a color that goes with your skin tone and lets your eyes shine through.

Eyeglasses are not just another accessory...they are actually vital to how effectively you will see the world and the way the world will see you! Glasses are a part of your basic wardrobe and need to complement your appearance and exemplify your personality and lifestyle.

The shape of the glasses should be determined by your facial shape. For example, a square facial shape might choose a round frame. Be aware that different shapes of frames are available in different sizes. The size of your face determines the size of your frame.

Skin tone is also very important in choosing eyeglasses. If you have yellow-toned skin, you need to choose warm shades like brown, gold and tortoise-shell frames. If you have blue undertones, you need to choose blue, plum and gray-black frames. To determine which skin tone you are, try both sets of colors on. The glasses should not wear you...the face should be in balance. If you have the incorrect shade of eyeglasses on, your skin will appear sallow. Ask your eyewear professional about color. They are normally trained in this. However, if you cannot find someone who can help you determine what color frame to get, consult an Image Consultant or Color Analyst.

Keep in mind the bridge of your nose. The three types of considerations are:

KEYHOLE

Keyhole fits a large nose.

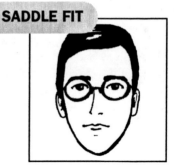

SADDLE FIT

Saddle fit looks like an inverted "U" and is suited for small to average nose size.

ADJUSTABLE

Adjustable nose pads can accomodate a fairly wide nose.

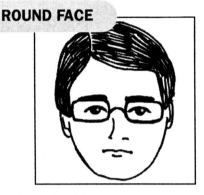

ROUND FACE

A round facial shape should choose a square or oval frame shape. Clear lower frames will give a lift to the face and will detract from the fullness.

SQUARE FACE

A square facial shape should choose round or aviator shape frames to soften the angles of the face.

LONG FACE

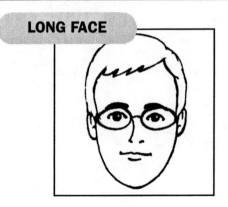

A long facial shape should choose a frame that is wider to soften the length of the face. Depending upon whether the face is oval or square, choose the appropriate opposite shape just right for you. Colored frames will give the illusion of breaking face length.

OVAL FACE

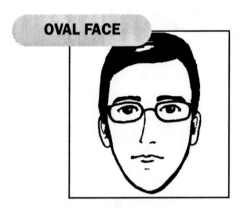

An oval facial shape can wear any type of frame unless the face is also long, in which case you should follow the guidelines for a long face.

Choosing eyeglasses is a matter of balance. Where you are wide, you want to take away from; where you are narrow, you will want to add to. Eyeglass frames should be as wide as the widest part of your face and in proportion to the shape and size of your face. Eyeglasses should "lift" your face by having an upward line or curve on the upper frame.

For good balance, your eye should be between the center and the top of the frame or lens. The lower frame should not repeat but complement your cheek and jawline. This means that you should not put round frames on a round face, or square frames on a square face.

Be sure to choose a high, slender, or rounded bridge for a small nose; a low, thick, or straight bridge for a longer nose. Plastic frames should blend with your complexion and hair coloring. A man with gray hair and cool-toned skin (blue undertones) looks much better in silver than gold eyeglass frames. A man with brown hair and warm-toned skin looks better in gold eyeglass frames.

SUNGLASSES

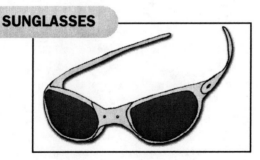

Selecting sunglasses follows the same rules as other eyewear, but you can vary by having them be more fun or extreme since they are a fashion accessory.

CONTACT LENSES

If you wear contact lenses, the smoked lenses are best. They do not distort your eye color but are easier to find when dropped. You will want to be careful about getting colored lenses as you do not want to look artificial.

TINTED GLASSES

You can get a light shading to your glasses if you like, such as one half to one point of color at the top to clear, or graduated, at the bottom lens. You might consider adding a soft tint at the lower outside corner of the lens. If you wear plastic lenses, this can be done to your existing glasses. A model's secret is that blue lenses tend to make the wearer squint from amplified intensity of the sunlight. Green and brown do not!

PHYSIQUE & SILHOUETTE

We are all unique. To do an analysis on your body type, you need to become an expert on yourself. NO BODY is perfect. Discover your body's proportions and learn the "art" of camouflage.

Chest size, waist and hips should be easy to determine by looking in a full length mirror. To determine if you have long legs, put a belt around your natural waist and see if you look high-waisted (not as much area above as below the waist). To determine if you have short legs, you would appear short-waisted in this experiment.

YOUR PERSONAL STYLE

Silhouette is what is important in developing your personal style. Silhouette describes the basic cut and shape of a garment, and this should be your main consideration when you go to purchase any suit, jacket or pant.

The clothes you choose should be right for you. If you choose clothing incorrectly, even you will realize it when you do not wear what you bought! Most people wear only 10% of what is in their closet because of clothing mistakes. We know when we put something on whether we like it on us, but in many cases, we do not know why.

THE FIT

Every man should look good in clothing. With the knowledge of what to do, as well as what not to do, this becomes very simple.

The following "rules" are myths:

- The only acceptable business shirt color is white.

- Tall men should stay away from plaids.

- Business men should only dress in dark colors.

- Men should not wear accessories.

- Men cannot have fun with their clothing.

- Heavy men should never wear a double breasted jacket.

- Short men should never wear double breasted jackets.

- Business men should wear a plain color tie, preferably blue.

Any man, regardless of body type, can dress well. However, to do so, you need to select your wardrobe with an eye for harmony, a sense of balance and proportion, and an awareness of each garment's individual silhouette.

A balanced silhouette can be achieved by paying attention to fit, color, and pattern. These three considerations determine the appropriateness of the two basic garments in the business wardrobe: the jacket and the pants, as well as necessary accessories.

The primary consideration, no matter what body type you are or how short or tall you are, is fit. Clothing creates an illusion by using the techniques of concealment and emphasis to achieve a desired image.

THE SHORT MAN

Usually, the legs are shorter than the upper torso. We want to create the impression that you have longer legs than you do. To do this, you need to "lift" the torso: raising the jacket by shortening at the bottom edge of the hem so it just covers the buttocks. When possible, buy a jacket marked S for short on the sleeve tag. You can also use a higher shoulder pad at the top of the jacket. These techniques "lift" the jacket and the silhouette will give the illusion that the added height is in the legs.

The waist of the jacket can also be indented or suppressed, and the sleeves should be short enough to show a reasonable amount of shirt sleeve, about 1/2 inch. This sleeve length will put your silhouette in balance and make the legs look longer. A two button jacket with a minimum of detail is a good choice for a short man. The more simple the details, the better.

Pants should be raised at the waist. Pants without cuffs are best, since cuffs shorten a leg. The hem should touch the vamp of the shoe in front and be angled downward so it is slightly longer at the heel, which keeps pant legs from touching the floor. Always be sure all sock area is covered. The pant legs should taper modestly from thigh to bottom to help give the illusion of a longer silhouette. The short man looks great in suspenders because the vertical line is increased and he can avoid wearing the "cutting in half" belt.

Accessories that should be avoided are bold patterns, which tend to overpower, horizontal lines, which interfere with the vertical look we are striving for, and heavy textures, which increase bulk and width. Instead, choose stripes and other vertical patterns for your best look.

THE TALL MAN

The tall man has length in his legs. You want to create a balanced silhouette. In contrast to the short man, who wants to stay away from horizontal lines, you will benefit from them! Tweeds and flannels and windowpane patterns will soften your tallness.

Pants should not be skimpy or too tight. Wearing pants too tight is

one of men's fashion misconceptions. The pants will be much more attractive if they fit well in a larger size. Jackets should have a slightly wider shoulder stance, and minimal shoulder pad, and the pants should be long enough to cover the buttocks.

Pants do not have to break over the shoe instep for a tall man, or be tapered or as high in the rise as with the shorter man, but rather should be cut fuller in the leg. A pleated front will also give the impression of fullness, as do cuffs.

Accessories can be bold with broader stripes on ties and shirts, a more obvious pocket square, and larger details. If you are tasteful and use these accessories to your advantage, these will give the illusion of proportion and you will appear a more average size.

THE HEAVIER MAN

The heavier man should avoid close-fitting clothes. Buy easy-fitting clothing that is comfortable in the chest, shoulder, and upper sleeve area.

Jackets should be of a smooth fabric. Bright colors and bold patterns will only increase bulk, so it is better to avoid these. More appropriate are darker colors, muted patterns, longer jackets, and few details. A ventless jacket has a slimming effect for the hips and pockets, and without flaps it can help to achieve a smooth look. A double breasted jacket, surprisingly enough, can be fitted on a heavier man, with style. This type of jacket has an asymmetrical line that distracts the eye away from the center of the torso. The single breasted jacket will tend to separate directly over the stomach and exposes and calls attention to the problem.

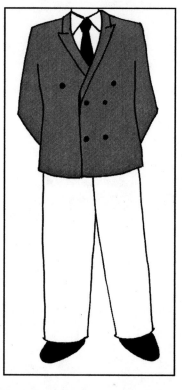

Pants should be trim, but not binding. The legs should taper slightly. If the fabric around the thigh measures 30", the knee would be about 26", and the bottom, 20". There should be no pocket flaps, heavy belts or ornate buckles. And please, wear the pants where they are intended to be worn—at the waist. Too often I see heavier men wearing their pants below their stomach, and this is not attractive. Single, inverted pleats are good and are less likely to wrinkle then outward facing pleats. Accessories should be subdued in color and design without being too small. The larger the man, the larger the collar and tie. Round faced men can look more angular by wearing a long-pointed collar and also can soften their appearance with round, club, or spread collars. The longer the neck, the higher the collar.

THE THIN MAN

The thin man wants to add bulk to balance his silhouette. Pants and jackets should be cut roomy enough, rather than too close to the body. Tweeds, twills and flannels are preferable. Small patterns, such as herringbone, add texture, warmth, and depth. Jackets need a fuller lapel,

pockets with flaps, and a shoulder line that extends out far enough so the shoulder tip is as wide as the thickest part of the upper arm. This gives the illusion of broader shoulders and a fuller chest and back. Pants should be pleated and cuffed and a belt can be bulky.

French cuffs add interest and bulk. A medium-width tie will add broadness, and a breast pocket handkerchief is great for width.

PERFECT BUILD

Few men have a perfect build. However, if you are in complete proportion, there are few rules you need to follow. Most clothing will look good on you. The face shape will still be a consideration in choosing eyewear and hairstyles.

ATHLETIC BUILD

Manufacturers have had to make adjustments in clothing due to the exercise and weight-building industry. Shop at a store that carries clothing designed for your specific need. A man with an athletic build has larger shoulders and a smaller waist and two-piece suits purchased in a regular department store would not be appropriate for this body type.

BUYING A SUIT

Now that you know your body type and shape, there are some options when buying a suit. What you will want to do is emphasize the positive and camouflage the negative.

The suit you buy will have a visual impact on your image. A man needs about five or six appropriate suits for business. The best suit colors are navy, blue, tan, and gray. A black suit is a must for formal wear. Purchase wool blends that can be worn all year and buy quality clothing always. Wool is a good investment because it lasts and can be worn all year. A good wool suit should last five or six years.

There is no formula for jacket length except that the buttocks must be covered in all cases. Knowing if you have short or long legs is helpful. For example, if you have short legs, you may want to have your jacket fall just at the curve of the buttocks. If you are tall, you may want to have the jacket fall a little lower to give the illusion of a better balanced silhouette. Be aware of different styles in coat vents.

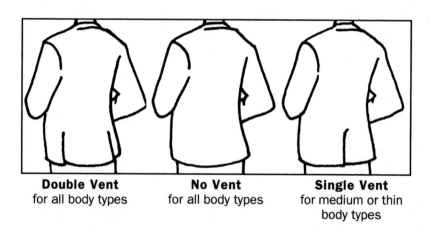

Double Vent
for all body types

No Vent
for all body types

Single Vent
for medium or thin
body types

FIT EVALUATION

A suit has to be comfortable. If you do not feel good in a suit, you will not look good. Try on each part of the suit separately before trying them on together. Follow these guidelines:

• Check the collar. Does it fit snugly across the neck?

• Do the lapels lay flat on your chest?

• Do the shoulders look natural on you?

• Does the back of the jacket fit snugly but not pull?

• Are the armholes loose enough for movement?

• Do the patterns match on the seams and armholes?

• Does the jacket cover the buttocks?

• Does the sleeve cover the writstbone and hit the top of the hand when the arm is bent?

• Does the jacket have an inside pocket?

• Do the buttons on the jacket match the color of the suit?

If you can answer yes to these questions, you have a good quality suit.

SUIT PANTS

The waistband should fall at the waist. The button at the top of the pants should fall at the navel for the correct fit. Cuffed pants are informal and should be avoided by men shorter than 5'8". If you are taller and choose to wear cuffs, they should be 1-1/2" deep and should be hemmed horizontally to the floor. Pants should measure about 19-1/4" around the knees and bottoms. They should not look tight in the crotch area. The bottom of the pants should cover the top half of the shoe.

VESTS

By wearing a vest you keep a finished look when you remove your suit jacket. A vest should be long enough to cover the waistband of the pant you are wearing. Be sure the vest gives you enough room and the buttons do not pull. The vest should be made of the same fabric as the suit. Vests look best on tall and thin men; however, if you choose one roomy enough, a vest can be worn on all body types.

INCORRECT

CORRECT

SHIRTS

A professional look requires a long-sleeved shirt with a sleeve length that puts the bottom of your shirt cuff level with the bottom of your jacket sleeve or no more than 1" below the jacket sleeve. The best fabrics are cotton or cotton blends. Shirt colors for business are solids, pale colors, or a thin pinstripe. Shirt collars are either straight or button-down. The button-down is more casual. The collar should be 2-1/2" to 3" from the fold to the point. The spread of the collar should be no more than 2-1/2".

Solid, cotton business shirt with straight collar. Note bottom of tie touches belt buckle for a correct look.

straight

button-down

The button-down collar is associated with the Ivy League look and complements the natural shoulder suit. It is appropriately worn with tweed sport jackets and woolen suits. This type of collar may also be worn with a bow tie to project a very professional image.

Since the button-down shirt is considered more casual, stay on the safe side if meeting with new clients and opt for a straight collar shirt. The straight point collar with medium points should be the basic staple of every man's wardrobe. This type of collar is appropriate for all suits.

TIES

A tie is the accessory that pulls a man's look together. It brings color to your outfit. Silk ties are the finest and most elegant. They will last and will update your wardrobe. Wear your tie correctly. Ties are available in different lengths, so be sure to match to your size. A tie should just touch your belt buckle (see illustration on previous page). Anything that differs in wrong. The tie does not belong above your waist or below!

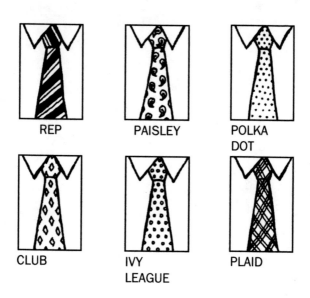

REP   PAISLEY   POLKA DOT

CLUB   IVY LEAGUE   PLAID

TIE DIMENSIONS

Ties vary from 2-1/2" to 3-1/2". As long as the proportions of men's clothing remain true to a man's body shape, this width will set the proper balance. Standard neckties come in lengths anywhere from 52" to 58" long. Taller men, or those who use a Windsor knot, may require a longer tie, which can be special-ordered. After being tied, the tips of the necktie should be long enough to reach the waistband of the pant.

Always confirm the appropriateness of the tie shape first and then feel the fabric. If it is made of silk and it feels rough to the touch, then the silk is of an inferior quality. Silk should feel soft to the touch. All fine ties are cut on the bias or across the fabric. This allows the tie to fall straight after the knot has been tied, without any curling.

Lining helps the tie keep its shape. The finest-quality ties are lined with 100 percent wool or silk.of a mixture. Normally, the higher the wool mixture, the higher the wool content. Be sure to check out the lining and the outer fabric, for the bulk of the tie should be the outer silk content and not the lining beneath.

Now look at the inverted V in your tie. In most quality ties, you will see a stitch joining the back flaps called the bar tack, which helps maintain the shape of your tie.

NECKTIE KNOTS

The standard way to tie a tie is the four-in-hand knot, the Windsor knot, or half-Windsor knot. The Windsor knot looks good with a spread collar. Ties should be tied so that there is a dimple or crease in the center of the tie just below the knot. This will force the tie to create fullness and drape correctly. Ask your sales representative when purhasing a tie to show you the proper way to do the four-in-hand and/or Windser knot.

Keep in mind the care your ties will require to hold their shape. You will be decreasing the longevity of your tie by pulling the small end out of the knot. Instead, untie the knot first, and reverse the steps you used when you put it on. This reversal of steps will untwist the fibers of the material and lining and help to alleviate light creases. A trick is to put the two ends of your tie togehter and roll the tie around your finger like you would a belt. Leave the tie in this shape overnight, then hang in your closet the next day. If your tie is knitted or crocheted, lay flat or rolled up instead and place it in a drawer.

COMBINING TWO PATTERNS WITH A SOLID

A rule of thumb is to combine one bold pattern with one subtle pattern. Avoid mixing same-scale patterns. A rep tie should be worn with a pinstripe shirt instead of a wide chalk stripe shirt. Similarly, a bold plaid jacket should be worn with a small pattern club tie rather than a paisley tie.

Make sure that all colors in the patterned pieces harmonize with each other. A brown suit with an orange pinstripe, for example, does not go with a red and brown tie.

With a bold plaid jacket and a solid color tie, the only permissible shirt patterns are a subtle pinstripe or a small, faint check. When wearing this jacket with a solid color shirt, complete the outfit with a tie that does not have an obvious directional pattern (i.e. club, dot, or ivy league).

Good two pattern combinations (third item is solid color) include:

• Pinstripe shirt with plaid, herringbone, or houndstooth check jacket.

• Pinstripe shirt with almost any tie pattern.

• Chalk stripe shirt with club, foulard, or pin dot tie.

• Box or windowpane check shirt with almost any tie pattern.

• Box or windowpane check shirt with tweed, pinstripe, or subtle plaid jacket.

• Tweed jacket with almost any tie pattern.

SUIT PATTERNS AND APPROPRIATE SHIRT AND TIE COMBINATIONS

PINSTRIPE

SHIRT: white solid
TIE: pin dot, stripe, foulard, paisley, solid (can be worn with striped shirt)

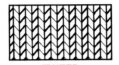

TWEED

SHIRT: white solid
TIE: stripe, foulard**, paisley, solid (can be worn with striped or tattersall shirt), club, plaid

HERRINGBONE

SHIRT: white solid
TIE: pin dot**, stripe, foulard**, paisley, solid (can be worn with striped, plaid* or tattersall* shirt), club, plaid

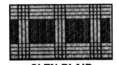

GLEN PLAID

SHIRT: white solid
TIE: stripe, foulard, club, solid (can be worn with striped shirt)

HOUNDSTOOTH

SHIRT: white solid
TIE: stripe, paisley, solid (can be worn with tattersall shirt), club, plaid

**for sport coat only
* for suit only

51

"A well-tied tie is the first serious step in life."

– Oscar Wilde

COMBINING THREE PATTERNS

Combining three patterns must be done with great care. A good guideline: do not wear three-patterned items unless one or more is extremely subtle. A very subtle pattern includes one that looks nearly solid.

Most three pattern combinations should include at least one pinstripe. Some examples that work are:

- Pinstripe suit, pinstripe shirt, club tie

- Glen plaid suit, small dot shirt, foulard tie

- Herringbone jacket, pinstripe shirt, rep tie

A monochromatic look (one color) works well if there is enough difference in shade among the three items. Contrast must be created between the shirt and the tie, and the shirt and the suit. One monochromatic outfit that works well is a charcoal gray suit, iced gray shirt, and medium gray tie. Varying the fabric texture also creates contrast. Consider, for example, a smooth worsted wool suit with an oxford cloth shirt and bulky knit tie.

Be careful when combining three different colors if the shirt is not white, off-white or beige. Wearing two shades of the same color plus a third color usually looks good, such as light pink and burgundy with gray. Some combinations of unrelated but harmonious colors mix well, but generally only when the shirt color is very pale. One example is a navy suit worn with a light yellow shirt and a wine colored tie. An outfit combining dark green, navy blue and brown, for example, obviously would not work!

Near-solids can be considered either a solid color or a patterned clothing item. A near-solid is a pattern so faint that the fabric has an overall solid appearance. Some pinstripes and tweeds fall into this category.

COMBINING TWO SOLIDS WITH A PATTERN

Coordinating one patterned item with two solids is usually easy. Any type or scale of pattern will work as long as the patterned item itself is appropriate for business wear (not a Hawaiian print shirt). All of the suit, shirt, and tie patterns illustrated can be combined with two solid color pieces.

A good general rule is to wear two contrasting solid color items (or strongly varying shades of the same color) and a patterned item that has one or both of the solid colors.

One example is a brown suit, a yellow shirt, and a yellow, blue, and brown paisley tie. Another combination that looks good is a brown suit, a tan shirt, and a blue and brown rep tie. An exception to this rule is when one of the solids is a white or near-white shirt; in this case, the colors of the tie and jacket need not overlap. An example would be a gray with silver pinstripe suit, white shirt and yellow tie.

The guidelines also apply when the outfit involves a sport coat and slacks rather than a suit. Three solids and one pattern follow the same rules. The slacks must coordinate with the rest of the outfit, and the color of the slacks can be matched by the patterned item.

DETAILS

Socks should be long enough to cover the skin when legs are crossed.

Tie width must be in proportion to collar size and lapel width. With wide jacket lapels, wear a shirt with long collar points and a moderately wide tie. Wear narrow ties with small collars and narrower lapels. Tie width and lapel width change with style and time periods.

A handkerchief worn in the jacket breast pocket should match one of the colors in an accompanying patterned tie. When worn with a solid color tie, the handkerchief can alternately pick up a background or thread color in the jacket.

COORDINATING SLACKS AND SPORT COATS

With solid color slacks, either a solid color or patterned sport coat is appropriate. A solid color sport coat should either be worn with a contrasting color slack or patterned slacks.

When combining a solid color sport coat with solid color pants, there are no hard and fast rules about what colors go together. It is generally correct to mix shades of the same color family, such as brown and beige, navy and medium blue, pearl gray, and charcoal gray. Almost any solid color sport coat will also work with neutral color slacks such as beige, tan, brown, gray, and navy, especially if you wear a patterned shirt or tie that has both colors to pull the outfit together.

With a patterned-solid combination, one of the colors in the patterned item should match the solid colored item, except when wearing a tweed jacket with neutral color slacks.

A solid color sport coat and patterned slack combination is always casual and should not be worn to work.

COMBINING SUIT AND SPORT COAT JACKETS, SHIRTS AND TIES

Mixing three solid color items is always safe. However, do create sufficient contrast to avoid looking too plain. A navy blue suit, white shirt, and maroon tie is always a great combination.

In constrasting clothing, there are these four things to keep in mind: LINE, COLOR, STYLE and TEXTURE.

pale blue tie	pale blue shirt	light gray suit	= INCORRECT
orange tie	green shirt	blue suit	= INCORRECT
red tie	brown shirt	green suit	= INCORRECT
maroon tie	**white shirt**	**dark blue suit**	**= CORRECT**

This is the formula to follow:

- solid suit with solid shirt and tie

- patterned shirt with solid tie

- solid shirt and patterned tie

- small pinstripe with patterned tie

- less is more in jewelry

- wear simple cuff links

- wear dark, over-the-calf socks

- wear a plain gold watch with gold or leather band

OFFICE IMAGE BASICS

- 2 suits, wool or wool blend—one dark color and one medium color

- 3 shirts, cotton or cotton blend—e.g., soft white, eggshell, gray

- shoes—black or brown wing tips

- plain tie with single dimples—2 conservative, always in silk

- belts—plain black or brown

- leather briefcase

- all-weather trench coat

SOCIAL IMAGE BASICS

- 2 sport coats—one wool tweed or patterned coat and one solid pant to match

- a separate pair of pants to match both sport coats—e.g., brown, gray, beige, blue

- 3 shirts, button-down collar—e.g., white, eggshell, blue

- 2 ties—one patterned, one solid

- one sweater vest or sweater to match sport coat and/or suit

- brown casual shoes—loafers in leather

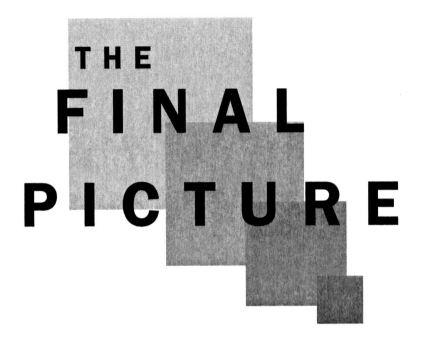

ACCESSORIES

HANDKERCHIEFS

Pocket squares can make an outfit complete. The best way to wear one is to hold the square up, grab the center, and push down into the pocket.

The handkerchief balances the colors of the tie and shirt. You can match it to your shirt or tie color even though it usually works better to match the tie. It is best that the handkerchief not be the same fabric or pattern.

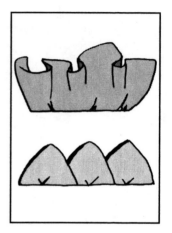

SHOES

The normal rule is that a shoe with a plain, smooth upper material and a thin leather sole is considered more dressy. Plain, smooth shoes look good with suits. A shoe with moderate design detail or texture on the upper and a medium leather sole can be worn for business and casual wear. Shoes reflect your taste and can tell a lot about the man who wears them.

Wear black shoes with blues, black or brown shoes with browns, and cordovans with browns and blues. The socks should match the shoes and pants and should always pick up some color, texture, or pattern from the shirt or tie. In business, ankle length socks are imperative. A man who pays attention to his clothing and accessories generally is a man who will pay attention to his work. He lets the world know he respects and knows quality.

PENNY LOAFER

WING TIP

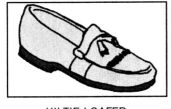

KILTIE LOAFER
WITH TASSEL

DRESS TIE

HOW TO BUY SHOES

Never buy shoes that do not feel right in the store. If they hurt your feet or do not feel comfortable in the store, they will probably not feel comfortable out of the store. Always shop for shoes at the end of the day when your feet are most spread. Even though you should buy the best shoes you can afford, this does not mean that the more expensive shoe is the better one.

When you shop, wear the sock that you intend to wear with the shoe you are purchasing.

Always have the salesperson measure both of your feet. This goes for the alterations person too. We do not have exactly the same size feet, arms or legs, in many cases. The ball of your foot should rest at the shoe's width and there should be approximately 1/2" between your largest toe and the end of the shoe. The arch of the shoe should match the arch of your foot for proper fit and support. If it does not, you may get blisters.

BELTS

Belts should be the same color as the pants and shoes. Narrow belts enhance short-waisted men and thicker belts enhance long-waisted men. If you want to balance a short waist and really lengthen your body, the secret is to wear your belt just slightly below your natural waistline.

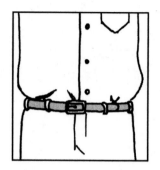

LEATHER GOODS

Your watchband, wallet, key case, briefcase, or notebook should coordinate with your clothing and usually are a dark neutral. Always use a gold or silver pen. The pen you pick up and the accessories you use "say" a lot about you.

SUSPENDERS

Suspenders are not for everyone. However, these look good under a vest and are especially attractive on a short man or a thin man. For a thin man, instead of calling attention to the man's thinness, the attention is on the pattern and width of the suspenders. On the other hand, a larger man can wear suspenders to use the vertical lines to make him appear thinner. Suspenders show a touch of style, individuality, and confidence.

JEWELRY

Keep your jewelry scaled to your size. Be aware of the "unwritten" dress code in your work setting. In a business setting, a gold watch, possibly cuff links, and a ring are sufficient.

SOCKS

Socks should always be over-the-calf to avoid any exposure of the leg. Appropriate colors are black, brown, and navy, for these go with most of your wardrobe. Wear white socks only for leisure. The best choice when choosing socks is cotton or a cotton mix.

YOUR PROFESSIONAL IMAGE

PERSONAL IMAGE

Many people believe that personal image is just about wearing the right clothes. Clothing is an essential part of nonverbal communication but not the only component. Many other factors are important to consider in order to achieve "polish" in your image. Paying attention to what is appropriate within your organization is crucial. Inappropriate clothing can send negative messages of indifference or disregard for others.

NONVERBAL COMMUNICATION

One of the ways we create our professional image is through nonverbal communication. This includes movement of a part of the body, such as a nod of the head or raising of the eyebrows or movement of the entire body, such as overall body tension or jumping up and down. It is not always easy to perceive various meanings of body language because this involves interpretation. If someone appears to you like they are upset, you may be interpreting that they are in a bad mood, while in reality, this look may be totally unintentional and that person may not be aware they look this way.

The study of body motion or kinesics involves the study of body movements in communication. It is estimated that the verbal part of some conversation accounts for less than 35% of social meaning of the conversation. Sixty-five percent is carried by non-speaking messages. This is what makes the understanding of nonverbal language so important. Body movement and positions can be considered either reflexive (involuntary) or non-reflexive. One reflexive indication is pupil dilation. At a Kinesics Convention, Dr. Edward H. Hess explained that clinical studies have shown that the pupil unconsciously widens when the eye sees something pleasant or exciting. Non-reflexive body language can be much more difficult to interpret. Many times, people can fake gestures. Look at a picture of yourself when you were genuinely happy and compare it to a posed picture. It is nearly impossible to hide how we are feeling. We believe in political leaders, actors, trial lawyers, and salespeople when they believe in themselves and this will come through in their body language.

PRACTICE THESE GUIDELINES... MAKE THEM HABITS!

- People who speak in a louder voice and those who speak more slowly are perceived to be more powerful and believable.

- The fewer hand and body gestures you make, the more powerful and intelligent you will appear to be.

- Leaders and powerful people take up more space than other people. They tend to lean slightly forward with their arms and legs relaxed and slightly spread. By taking up more space, they appear to be taking charge.

- The person that has a high eye level is usually perceived as the leader. People tend to address that person first.

- Smiling makes a person seem friendly and more attractive.

- There are no gender differences with handshakes. Shake hands with confidence.

- Become aware of your energy and other people's energy.

- Stand casually with good posture and keep in good body alignment.

Most nonverbal messages of dress are unintentionally communicated and unintentionally received. For example, if you are dressed in jeans and a T-shirt, other people may unconsciously think you are not a professional person or that you have a low academic background.

Knowing and understanding the effect clothing has on people will give you power and will reduce the number of messages that are unintentionally sent and received. To have effective communication, both the sender and the receiver need to be consciously aware of what messages are being sent.

Clothing is a language. The wearer gives a message which is transmitted by clothing through a visual channel which is decoded by another person. The perceptions of the person receiving the information or the person who is observing it is what matters. McGraw discovered that the self-esteem of the wearer is involved in this decision:

"When you know who you are, then you know how you look. All these little extras just fall into place. You learn about your body. When people present themselves physically, you can tell how they feel about themselves."

Dress codes in business are based on the assumption that the perceptions of the public are most important. The research findings indicate that perceptions are made and in most cases represent stereotypes about clothing, A police officer gets compliance from citizens because of his uniform. A nun demands respect and compliance due to her habit. Dress does have an effect on people. Graduates wear clothing that signifies achievement. People respond to clothing messages. Some of the things clothing "communicates" are whether you are powerful or not powerful, credible or non-credible, trustworthy or not trustworthy, aggressive or passive, or likeable or not likeable. People can determine by looking at your clothing things like your economic status, social status, and degree of professionalism. Most of all, what you choose to wear tells people how you feel about yourself. Clothing also affects your behavior. If you wear something you like, you will get a psychological lift and perform better.

It is not by accident that people are powerful. They submit to the paradigm. "If you fail to plan, you plan to fail." They know what they want and they learn the steps necessary to reach their goal. They tend to be organized. As a behavior and values counselor, I've observed hundreds of powerful people and found that these people were dominant and individualistic in nature and knew exactly what they were doing and where they were going. These people, while appearing to be somewhat relaxed, were very uptight. They have a goal and they will do whatever they have to get to the goal. They will dress the part, act the part, be the part. They will emulate successful people. They will learn from successful people. They will learn to talk like successful people. They learn the power position, such as standing with perfect posture and poise, standing erect and spreading their feet slightly. They hire professionals and mentors to inform them on how to be their best.

To accomplish the "look" of a power person, it is necessary to be "an expert on yourself." A full-length mirror to see yourself as others see you and an audio tape player to hear yourself as others hear you are good first steps. If you have video tapes you have been in, these can be helpful tools for evaluating how you look to others. The goal is to determine your sense of presence.

The power look has always consisted of the traditional suit, white shirt and fine accessories. Finding your individual style is discovering your uniqueness. To project a powerful image requires that you package yourself appropriate to your profession. Although diet and exercise can help to reshape your body, you are who you are through genetics. Some people are short, some tall, some thin, and some stocky. If your shoulders are broad and thin, if your arms are short or long, this is not going to change! Your silhouette is what is important in determining your body type. A silhouette describes the basic cut and shape of a garment and this needs to be your main consideration when purchasing clothing.

Personal grooming is just as important as what you wear. Improper grooming will ruin any image you work to project.

COMPONENT	GROOMING
Hair	Clean, trimmed, and neatly arranged.
Facial Hair	Shaved, neatly trimmed. Trim nose hair and hair on ears.
Nails	Neat, clean and trimmed
Teeth	Brushed, no gaps.
Breath	Tobacco, alcohol, and coffee have odors—avoid these
Body	Bathed, showered—use deodorant
Cologne	Use sparingly, or not at all

PSYCHOLOGY OF COLOR

When you see lights flashing, a siren blasting or a red fire truck, you react. Color does affect the emotions and symbolizes many things for people. People choose their clothing and accessories according to their taste in color. Color surrounds us. Technology makes it possible for so many colors and prints to choose from. At one time, the color purple was available only to royalty because of the exclusiveness of the dye. People respond strongly to color.

The three primary colors are red, yellow, and blue. These three colors plus black and white form all other colors. Primaries and combinations of two primaries create color families (hues), which bring about reds, oranges, yellows, greens, blues, and purples. All colors involve temperature (warm or cool undertones), depth (lightness or darkness) and intensity (brightness) or quiet nature of a color.

Psychologists say that color means different things to different people. It is believed that color aesthetics are learned, and that they are somewhat cultural. Color can stimulate, excite, depress, soothe, and affect your state of mind. Psychologists have demonstrated in laboratories that warm colors such as orange-red, yellow, and orange can raise blood temperature and stimulate appetite. Red can step up your heartbeat, and blue can slow it down. Think of "seeing red" when you are upset and "feeling blue" when you are down.

It would be a good idea to have a professional work with you to see what colors will bring out your best.

Mens Dress Guide

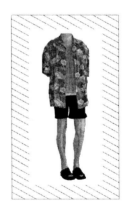

Casual		Formal
Daily		Social
Power		Inappropriate

OFFICIAL DRESS GUIDE

It is recognizable that dress and image are important. Standards for dress codes are already in place of hundreds of occupations. Businesses recognize that dress and image has an effect on people. This effect can be negative or positive. A dress code establishes a sense of unity among employees within an occupation. Although dress codes may set a limit on personal choice, conforming to an established dress code offers the advantage of working in a team environment within a larger organization that symbolizes the importance of the company. Customer research has found that certain clothing choices denote professionalism, dedication, and pride for the company for which one works. The old adage, "You don't get a second chance to make a good first impression" is still true. In and out of the workplace, men and women will be judged by their clothing communication.

The basic business suit is still the acceptable norm for both the power and daily business attire. Even though business casual has been implemented in many places of business, when you have a client meeting scheduled, the client comes first. They need to feel comfortable with you. When meeting with clients out of the office, regular business attire is what is appropriate (suit, tie) unless the company you represent has in place a business casual policy and you are invited to participate in their policy. For meetings in the office, your dress should be appropriate to your clients' expectations. Keep in mind that without clients there is no business. The clothing you choose to wear can and will have an effect on your customer.

SIX CATEGORIES OF DRESS

The following categories will help you to "package" yourself for your particular occupation. Different careers have different wardrobe needs. In banking, accounting and law, this would be a classic suit. In retail, education and sales, suits or sport coats can work, and in construction, jeans are suitable. In the field of entertainment, art, fashion, and interior design, an unconstructed suit may be warranted.

POWER DRESS

Your suit needs to fit as it were made for your body. A power suit is always custom-made. This suit is intended to make a strong visual impact on your business image. If you choose to wear a double-breasted suit, the buttons must stay buttoned and should match the color of the suit. Unless you have a derriere that is in direction proportion with the rest of your body, always opt for a side vent jacket. A vest will provide a finished look and should be the same fabric as the suit. The vest always covers the waistband of your pant and just barely shows above your suit lapel.

Professional businesses that are traditional such as banks, insurance companies, legal, accounting firms, stockbrokers, and government wear two-piece single-breasted wool in a medium weight fabric, suit and suit pant. A crisp white long-sleeved shirt, silk tie or scarf tied with some background color, and leather accessories are crucial.

DAILY DRESS

If you want a job, you have to look the part. Dressing successfully will enable you to get that promotion, earn that respect, and move up the corporate ladder. The most important wardrobe item is the business suit. Buy the best you can afford. Wool or wool blends are a must in a business wardrobe.

The traditional colors of a suit for men are charcoal, medium gray, navy blue, medium blue, khaki/tan, olive green and tweed textured.

Shirts for men are traditionally white, pale blue, pale pink, blue striped with a straight collar, and french-cuff.

The best tie colors for traditional business wear are red, dark blue, teal, purple, olive, and taupe. Traditional dressing requires fine accessories, such as leather belts, line handkerchiefs, small cuff-links, gold watch, and leather shoes.

Businesses that involve manual labor and office activity, such as engineering, manufacturing, or transportation allow for a more relaxed daily dress requirement. You should always dress business-like and avoid extremes in your personal appearance, such as beards, ponytails, braids, or earrings. Shirts should have a collar and pants, shoes, and socks should be appropriate.

Creative environments such as retail, decorating, cosmetic companies, and publishing require a wool two-piece suit with some flair, such as a pocket square.

CASUAL DRESS

The casual trend began in 1990 in Canada when many companies introduced a dress-down day as part of their annual Fall United Way Campaign.

• *About 15 million of the 118 million employees in American work-places dress casually at work.*
• *About 90% of Americans wear casual clothes to work at least some of the time.*
• *Fifty-three percent of white-collar workers are allowed to dress casually every day, a 20% increase from 1995. And 90% of all US Business has a casual business wear policy.*

– Levi Strauss and Company

One of the reasons market researchers say that companies have moved toward casual business wear is due to baby-boomers, who grew up in jeans and never wanted to wear the gray flannel suit. What you wear to work influences how people will treat you. What you wear will affect your professionalism and how people will perceive you. Since you have to go to work anyway and you have the option of appearing professional and competent, isn't it better to look professional and either stay in your current position or move up the corporate ladder? Most of the time, even with casual days in effect in many of our corporations, we believe, and research shows, that most of the time you should still wear traditional clothing meant for work. If you look at successful men and women, you will notice they choose dark, solid colors for their wardrobes and always wear suits.

In today's competitive workplace, whether it is technological, service, or retail, it is now more important than ever to dress appropriately for your job. Casual dress was created to take the image of rigid gray flannel suits to a more creative and entrepreneurial dress with the purpose of combining power suit authority with comfort. The gray flannel suit of the 1950's imposed conformity thought necessary at the time in corporations. Today's corporations are changing. There is downsizing, mergers, acquisitions, and change in management on a regular basis. There are many jobs available, and people are thinking about changing to a company that can offer them what they are looking for. There are young people in their twenties who are working from their homes and producing Fortune 500 companies. For these people, clothing is not an issue. However, when they go out to represent their service or product to a client, they will need to know about the appropriate dress code to succeed. Casual dress is about comfort, neatness, and professionalism.

What is right for casual days for a computer guru is just not right for an accountant's office. It may be that a blazer or casual pantsuit are as casual as your company may want.

Your clothes must work with your market, your environment, your clients, and your colleagues. By knowing how your business associates dress and observing how you expect the people they meet to dress is critical. It is okay to ask them what they deem appropriate for your particular business.

It is important to make others feel comfortable. You need to know where you are going and how to practice business etiquette, which is to observe clothing customs. You must fit into your client's culture. If you have a relaxed dress code in your office, keep a blazer and dress blouse and appropriate shoe in your office. You never know when the senior vice-president will decide to see how your department is doing.

Bob Dole was betrayed by the bagginess of his suit and a personal style that only asked people to listen to his speech, not connect with his vision, according to personal presentation experts. His message was, "I am a stern parental figure."

Recruiters assume how you look at your interview will be the most professional you will ever look.

APPROPRIATE BUSINESS CASUAL

- Coordinated Clothing
- Navy Blazer
- Khaki Pants
- Sweaters
- Pressed, well-fitted Pants
- Polo Shirts
- Sport Shirts
- Cotton Shirts

INAPPROPRIATE BUSINESS CASUAL

- T-shirts of any kind
- Jeans of any kind
- Sandals
- Shorts
- Worn or torn clothing
- Weekend clothing
- Stained clothing
- No socks

SOCIAL DRESS

It is very different when you choose social dress for a work environment. When dressing socially, it is not imperative that you wear a suit and tie and you can choose a comfortable shoe; however, you should ALWAYS have fine fabrics and look your best. A social occasion gives you the opportunity to show your individuality.

FORMAL DRESS

Formal dress is the ultimate in dressing. This is the time for long gowns for women and tuxedos for men.

INAPPROPRIATE DRESS

Inappropriate dress in a professional setting would include jogging wear, shorts and T-shirts. Skin should not be showing. Avoid excessive jewelery, and always wear socks.

REMEMBER TO USE THE "COST-PER-WEAR" FORMULA!

The true cost of anything that you buy is not the amount you actually paid. It is the number of times you ultimately wear it. Therefore, an expensive garment may be a lifetime investment if you wear it often.

EXAMPLE:
1 business suit bought for $500
            worn 25 times
            costs $20 each wearing

I firmly believe that what gives other people a sense of what and who they are in is the way they are dressed. It is the first impression. I can't think of a man, who, whether in business or leisure, does not want to project authority.

— Bill Blass

BUSINESS GUIDELINES FOR MEN

	POWER	DAILY	SOCIAL	CASUAL	INAPPROPRIATE
JACKETS	tailored fitted natural fibers	tailored fitted natural fibers	tailored fitted natural fibers	no sport coat long sleeve shirts	jogging wear
PANTS	tailored, fitted pant for suit	tailored, fitted pant for suit	tailored, fitted pant for suit	fine denims soft fabrics	shorts
SHIRTS	tailored white cotton	tailored white cotton	tailored white cotton	collarless long sleeves	t-shirts skin showing
ACCESSORIES	solid small stripe leather belt plain socks	solid small stripe leather belt plain socks	solid small stripe leather belt plain socks	no tie loafers	excess jewelry no socks

MEN'S WARDROBE

- Four or five suits—solid blue or gray, navy, patterned, pinstripe, or glen plaid.

- Three blazers/sport coat—blue, navy, or camel

- Six pants

- Nine shirts - 3 white, 3 blue, three pattern—all long sleeved.

- Six ties—solids, stripes, and patterns. Ties should always fall at the top of your belt buckle.

- Two sweaters

- One raincoat—black or brown

- One overcoat—navy, black, or brown

- Three pairs of shoes—wing tip, lace, loafer

- Dark leather briefcase

- Gold watch—classic roman numeral

- Belts—keep dark leathers—no ornate buckles

- 12 pair of socks—dark solids in medium tones. Always above the calf. Argyles for casual only.

- 1 pair leather gloves

- Glasses to match hair tone

Self respect cannot be hunted. It cannot be purchased. It is never for sale. It comes to us when we are alone, in quiet moments, in quiet places, when we suddenly realize that knowing the good, we have done it, knowing the beautiful, we have served it, knowing the truth, we have spoken it.

— Whitney Griswold

When we think of Image, what comes to mind is our outer appearance—how we appear to others. But, what about the "inside?" Is it really true that "It's not what's on the outside that counts?" While it is true that we are judged in a very short period of time on our outer appearance, and that accounts for much of an impression that is made, there needs to be a balance between what we appear to be on the outside and what we actually are on the inside.

Beauty today has a new definition. In the 1800's beauty meant something to be looked at, admired, copied, or painted. These are superficial qualities. Beauty today has an inward feeling—a total experience for both men and women emotionally, psychologically, and aesthetically. It is actually being in control and being challenged. If you feel beautiful you will feel confident, relaxed, and ready for anything that requires your performance. Beauty should not lie in the eyes of the beholder, but in the heart of the possessor. In the story of *The Ugly Duckling* by Hans Christian Anderson, when the duckling had been convinced by everyone that he was ugly, nothing seemed to go right. But, when he saw a true reflection of himself he rejoiced from his heart, "I never dreamed of so much happiness when I was the ugly duckling." Beauty brings confidence and confidence is the magic behind what it takes to be successful in both your personal and/or professional life.

Do you see yourself as a "victim?" Do you blame people for what happens in your life? Are you positive towards other people or do you have negative feelings toward them? Only when you understand the answers to these questions will you be able to succeed in life and become a person who is whole from Head to Soul.

The next time you have trouble falling or staying asleep or you cannot concentrate on something someone is saying, think about the conversation you are having within yourself and try to make yourself aware of your inner voice. Who is talking within you? Do you have feelings that you have not worked through? Talk out loud and discover how to remedy this situation. Perhaps you are thinking about an upcoming assignment at work and it is keeping you up at night or someone in your family said something to you and you just cannot get it out of your mind. Dr. Frederick Perls, a Freudian analyst, used this principle to invent Gestalt Therapy.

Gestalt is a German word that means an organized whole. He perceived that many personalities lack wholeness and have fragmented personalities. He felt people are often aware of only parts of themselves instead of their whole self. The purpose of this type of therapy was to help people to become whole and to help them to become aware of, admit to, reclaim, and bring together their fragmented parts. A person needs, he felt, to be self-sufficient and have an inner support system within their soul and not need to receive this from any other source.

There are many people who feel they need another person to be whole. We have all heard in introductions, "This is my other half," or "This is my better half." If we are to develop on the inside, then it is very important that we are self-reliant. This interprets into not having the need to depend on a significant other, job title, academic achievement, or bank balance to feel whole in your soul. Your capabilities of what you can do and who you are should be internal in the knowledge that you can depend always on you.

Perl suggests you use the word "I" instead of the word "it" in order to assume responsibility for your behaviors. He developed what is known today as the "chair technique" whereby you have two chairs opposite one another and you sit in one chair and communicate your thoughts and then sit in the other chair and communicate back to yourself. This "hot seat" method was used with a teacher in his study who thought of herself as friendly but did not understand why she did not have any close friends. She empathically denied any angry feelings, though others described her as an angry person. When the teacher roleplayed her fragmented self, she acted her friendly self from the hot seat and imagined her angry self on the opposite chair. The dialogue went something like this:

"I don't know why I'm here. I'm always so nice."
"You do know why you are here. You don't have any close friends."
"I don't understand. I'm always trying to help people."
"That's the problem. You're always helpful and people feel obligated to you."

Within a short time, the teacher heard herself getting loud and realized her anger. She was now ready to admit that she could be so angry.

The LikeAbility Profile™

What is your self image?
Do you like yourself?
Take the LikeAbility Profile™ and find out!

1. Are you a friend of yours?

2. Do you greet people with a smile, give your hand, look them in the eye and give your name with pride?

3. When you answer the telephone, do you answer it with a smile and give your name?

4. Do you invest in your own special knowledge?

5. Do you always say "thank you?"

6. Do you accept compliments well?

7. Do you keep your problems to yourself unless they directly relate to the situation?

8. Do you consciously try not to make excuses to people?

9. Can you avoid bragging about yourself?

10. Do you accept you for who you are?

11. Do you enjoy your life?

12. Do you look at unsuccessful experiences as opportunities to learn and change?

13. Do you look at ridicule as ignorance?

14. Do you handle constructive criticism well?

15. Do you enjoy doing things for yourself, without feeling guilty?

16. Can you adapt to stressful situations?

17. When you make comments to yourself, are they of a positive nature?

18. Do you seek out positive and successful, motivated people to associate with and use as role models?

19. Do you want to be involved and contribute something to this world?

20. Do you want to be important?

21. Are you an honest person?

22. Are you a sincere person?

23. Are you a sensitive person?

24. Do you have the best posture for your anatomical structure?

25. Are you open to new ideas and to other peoples' opinions? Are you able to see the "other side?"

26. Do you have a sense of humor?

27. Do you stand up for yourself?

28. Do you have good listening skills?

29. Do you like to learn?

30. Do you like yourself?

Evaluation

- If you answered no to less than 3 or 4 questions, you are exteremely likeable and are very close to being the best person one can be.

- If you answered no to less than 8 questions, you are still likeable, but need to consider turning more negatives into positives.

- If you answered no to more than 8 to 10 questions, you should probably re-evaluate yourself, your life and your goals.

Take this profile periodically to re-evaluate after self improvement is realized.

One of the most important elements of success is self awareness. It is the ability to step back from life and take a good look at who you are and how you relate to your environment. It is the ability to accept yourself as a unique individual and to be able to recognize your potential, as well as your limitations.

Self awareness is being honest in what you see, knowing your strengths and weaknesses, knowing what you can contribute and recognizing that both time and effort will be necessary to achieve this. A winner will be able to look in the mirror and like what they see. A winner tries all through life to be the very best in thought, word, and deed.

This instrument is a self-awareness tool to be used for measuring LikeAbility. If you do not like yourself, you'll have difficulty accepting other peoples' love. Next to psychological, safety and social needs are the need to be someone and to feel that you have something to contribute. This is called self-actualization and according to Maslow is the ultimate need. Socrates says, "Know thyself."

ATrademarked creation fromThe ImageMaker, Inc.
www.imagemaker1.com

Do you know someone who lights up a room when he or she enters? Or a person who seems comfortable with everyone they meet? The type of person who knows how to make others feel comfortable is a person who feels comfortable within. This is someone who has charm.

Charm is a glow within a woman that casts a most becoming light on others.

– John Mason Brown

Charm is the ability to be friendly, energetic, kind, and caring whatever the circumstances. It is an attitude toward yourself, toward others, and toward the world in which you live. Charm comes from within. "Smile, and the world smiles with you." A smile gives a silent message that says, "I am approachable, and I like you." People will respond favorably to people they like, and people like people who like them. The person who smiles has made the other person feel comfortable.

CARING
Caring comes from within. It is important to care about yourself but also important to care about others. You receive a strong feeling of self-satisfaction when you care for others and what you give to others will reap an added benefit for you if you ever need someone to care about you.

ETIQUETTE
Etiquette is also an inner quality. You show you care about yourself by understanding the importance of good manners. It does not cost anything to be pleasant. A person who cares about himself or herself also cares about others. A simple "thank you," "you're welcome," "I'm sorry, I was wrong," or "excuse me" are cleansing words. By writing a thank you note or giving someone a remembrance are simple and thoughtful ways that will provide you with inner serenity and confidence as a human being.

In nothing do we lay ourselves so open as in our manner of meeting and salutation.

– Lavater

BUSINESS AND SOCIAL ETIQUETTE

INTRODUCTIONS

It is important to always identify yourself and to introduce others. If you cannot remember a name, say "I'm sorry, would you mind telling me your name again?" Then, proceed with the introduction. If you perceive that someone does not remember your name, graciously supply it to prevent any embarrassment.

Always introduce a younger person to an older person.

"Mrs. Brown, I'd like you to meet Jane Adams."

Introduce one person to a group stating the newcomer first, then other names in order of position, if applicable, around the room. Always look at the person you are introducing and be confident and in control.

The most important person is always mentioned first.

"Mr. Smith, this is Miss Jones, our new district manager."

Men are introduced to women except when the man is holding a higher ranking. Women should be presented to Ambassadors, Clergy and Presidents.

"Mr. President, may I present Mrs. Jane Thompson."

In a formal introduction, introduce a man to a woman.

"Michelle Day, this is Tom Gilligan."

There are no gender differences in business. Family and relatives are introduced informally.

"You've met my husband, Alan."

RESPONDING TO AN INVITATION

One word answers are not appropriate. They could make other people uncomfortable. Always repeat the person's name to help you remember and to be polite. Use phrases such as "Jackie and I went to the same law school." Let people know that you are interested enough to say a few things and help them feel comfortable.

"Hello Mary, I've looked forward to meeting you. I've heard so much about you."

Avoid a phrase like "Not bad, I hope!"

TELEPHONE SAVVY

Always identify yourself when you call. People are busy and sometimes may not recognize your voice. Never expect someone to remember your name or put them in that uncomfortable position.

Politely ask "May I speak to?" Do not say "Who is calling?" Instead say "May I please tell ____ who is calling?" Always keep pencil and pen by the telephone you will be using. This is respecting peoples time. Always use a pleasant telephone voice. It is the first impression you will be making for the company your work for. Never yell for someone besides yourself to come to the telephone.

Hand the telephone up gently and always ask the person you are calling if this is a good time for them to talk. If you dial an incorrect number, apologize and ask whether you have dialed correctly by repeating the number you called.

Try looking in a mirror while talking on the telephone. It shows you how you sound and will add enthusiasm and confidence to your voice.

IMPRESSIONS

Keep in mind that it takes 5 seconds to make an impression, 21 days to start a pattern, 100 days to become automatic, 30 days to forget a message. In 24 hours, 66% of your message is lost. It takes 8 days of constant reminding to have 90% retention rate in a 30 day period.

TABLE ETIQUETTE

Never start eating until everyone has been served, unless the host tells you to begin. Do not pour wine until everyone at your table is seated. It is appropriate for either gender to pick up the check. The determining factor is who extended the invitation.

The tableware is set up for you to work from left to right. Your setting normally would consist of napkin, dinner fork, salad fork, dinner plate, knife and soup spoon, provided all these courses are being served. The cutting edge of the knife blade should be turned in toward the plate. Silverware for dessert may be brought to the table with dessert placed above the dinner plate, parallel to the edge of the table. If using a spoon, the bowl goes to the left; if using a fork, tines go to the right. A dessert spoon may also be placed next to the knife. (Spoons used to stir coffee or tea are usually brought to the table with the beverage). At the top of the place setting, water glasses go to the right, directly above the knives. Wine glasses go to the right of water glasses, slightly near to the edge of the table. Bread and butter plates go directly above the fork with the butter knife set across the place. Bread is broken off and eaten one piece at a time. Salad plates should be positioned to the left of the napkin and fork. The host will begin to eat first.

Some rules to follow are:
- Never dunk
- Chew with the mouth closed.
- Eat fried chicken with a knife and fork, unless you are at a picnic.
- If a business occasion, the conversation should focus on business.
- Spoon away from you.
- If soup bowl has handles, you may drink.
- If you are in an interview, only order one drink.
- Never turn your glass upside down to decline drinks.

- Never wave silverware when talking.
- Never write on the tablecloth.
- Pass food to your right.
- Pass liquids and gravies with ladle.
- Pass salt and pepper together.
- If you spill something, use your napkin, but never dip into your water glass.
- Do not use toothpicks.
- Wear a smile at the table.
- Do not reach, ask.
- If you spill something on someone else, offer your napkin if clean.
- If something drops from the table, let the wait staff pick it up.
- Cut fruit before eating.
- If you must remove something from your mouth with your fingers, place it on the edge of your plate.
- Blow your nose quietly without excuse.
- Pat the area around your mouth with your napkin instead of wiping across your mouth.
- Do not smoke.
- Sticky foods, such as cake, are eaten with a fork, as are french fries.
- Ask to be excused when finished. Thank the person who asked you or made the meal.
- Dessert is ordered only after the main course.
- When your glass is half empty, stop drinking and wait for a refill.
- If you use sugar, place the empty wrapper under your plate.
- Try and leave a small portion of food on your plate.
- Never push or move your plate, stack plates, or hand your plate to the server.
- Make your decision for your order in a timely manner.
- Leave your problems at home.
- Watch voice quality.
- Be on time.
- Be kind to restaurant personnel.

HARD TO EAT FOODS

Asparagus—Cut off the soft top part with a fork and eat. Cut stem with knife and fork.

Lobster—Request the lobster be cracked. Use the fork provided. Crack claws with tool and break apart with hands. Cut large pieces into small bites.

Chicken—Eat with knife and fork, one bite at a time.

Artichokes—Pull off one leaf and dip in sauce.

Snails—Pick up shell with napkin or tool and lift out with a fork.

Seafood—Ask the waitress to bone the fish or open with fork and knife and remove. Discard on your plate to the side.

Spaghetti—Cut a few strands and wind around your fork. Take the spoon in your left hand and the fork in your right and roll noodles into a ball. No ends should be shown. You can also use a fork to wind the noodles with the help of a spoon.

Fruit—Pick up with fingers and dip in sauce. Eat juice in the fruit with a spoon.

ETIQUETTE ONE-LINERS

"May I?" Implies the person has authority.

"As you of course know..." Affirmation that this person has great knowledge of the subject.

"I'd like your advice..." You recognize superior wisdom and value their opinion.

"I'd sure appreciate it if..." Implication that he has the power to grant or refuse.

"You are so right..." Who won your last argument? Everyone wants to be right.

"Can you possibly spare time from your busy schedule..." Recognition of their time.

"A person of your standing..." You are saying they are a pro.

"I'm sorry you feel that way..." Takes power back from negativity.

ETIQUETTE KNOW HOW

• Yelling is never productive.
• Use hand, head, and facial gestures.

- Name badges are won on the right so the eye will focus when shaking hands.
- After any interview, send a thank you note ASAP.
- Say Please, You're welcome, Excuse me, I'm sorry where applicable.
- Never interrupt.
- Talk about ideas, not people.
- Avoid any arguments.
- Do not tuck ear or chin or pull on face.
- Do not toe tap, nail tap, or pencil tap.
- Do not talk too much or too loud.
- Do not swing your foot.
- Do not twist your hands.
- Do not crack your knuckles. It's like chalk on a chalkboard for many people.

POSTURE & BODY LANGUAGE

Posture and Body Language exhibit inner confidence. Good posture "says" to others, "I feel good about myself." What we say with our hands, eyes, eyebrows, walk, and facial expressions often speaks louder than any words or sentences we use. Keep in mind that body language is an extremely important tool. Statistics have shown that we are being judged mostly on our outer body appearance. This is known as nonverbal communication. A true understanding of how we appear to others can make it easier to send more effective messages.

WHAT THEY DO	WHAT THEY "SAY"!
raised eyebrows	surprise, questioning
shaky hands	uneasy, uncomfortable
tapping feet	nervous, hurried
limp handshake	lack of confidence
lowered chin	shy

It is important to know that what you do may result in others thinking something entirely different from what you intended your message to be!

For you to be the best you can be, you must possess the ingredients for a beautiful inner personality to shine through. What you are on the inside is crucial to making the outside appearance work for you. Have you ever had a friend who was a wonderful person but did not consider outside appearance a priority for them? Or did you have a friend that looked great all of the time but did not possess those inner qualities? Imagine giving each friend the "balance ingredient" for total success.

Outer Appearance + Inner Qualities = Total Beauty

Yes, it is true that what is on the outside does count but the really important things in life are not found on the outside of our bodies. Qualities such as kindness, caring, and love make people happy and confident. Although we are judged on what people see, and this will "open doors" for you, once you go through that door, you need to continue to make a positive impression—a lasting impression that makes others comfortable being with you.

Image is a total process by which you develop your look on the outside have your own individual style. Then you work to develop your inner self to achieve happiness and self-confidence.

You cannot be useful to someone else unless you have identified "who you are." There are instruments that measure behavior and values that do this.

It takes courage and commitment to experience the freedom of being whole, to take a stand on something you believe in, to say to your significant other or a colleague, "I'm sorry you feel that way." It takes courage and belief in yourself to choose being authentic over receiving approval. The saying, "It's lonely at the top" is true if you allow it to be. You must accept responsibility for your own choices. As long as you feel in your heart that you do the "right thing," you will have the courage to not allow yourself to be influenced by outside forces.

Consider the following "keys for success":

• Look at where you are now. Where would you like to be?

• What will it take to reach your goal?

• Remember that you create you own success. Rid yourself of any negative thoughts.

• What type of roadblocks are keeping you from the success that you deserve?

If you have the courage you will reach self-actualization and experience a feeling only a self-actualized person can feel. It is a feeling of wholeness from the inside out—From Head to Soul.

Image is a total process by which you develop your look on the outside and have your own individual style. Then you work to develop your inner self to achieve happiness and self-confidence. A person who has mastered the art of total image is a person who has inner and outer qualities. It is a person who is beautiful from the inside out.

Set the course of your life by the three stars - sincerity, courage and unselfishness. From these flow a host of other virtues...He who follows them will obtain the highest type of success: that which lies in the esteem of others.

— Dr. Monroe E. Deutch

Success breeds success...and more success and more success!

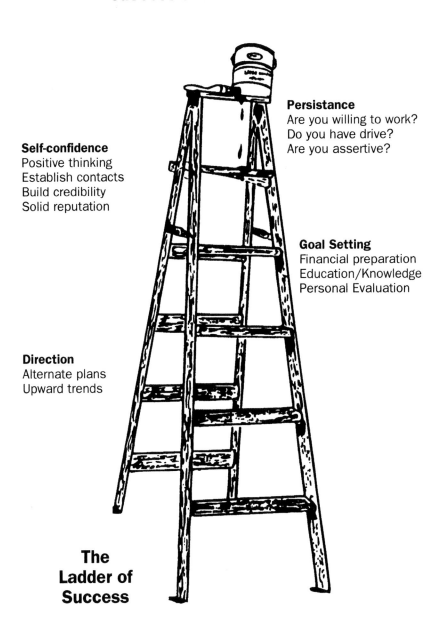

Persistance
Are you willing to work?
Do you have drive?
Are you assertive?

Self-confidence
Positive thinking
Establish contacts
Build credibility
Solid reputation

Goal Setting
Financial preparation
Education/Knowledge
Personal Evaluation

Direction
Alternate plans
Upward trends

The Ladder of Success